50 ONE-MINUTE TIPS FOR TRAINERS

A QUICK AND EASY GUIDE

Carrie A. Van Daele

A FIFTY-MINUTE™ SERIES BOOK

CRISP PUBLICATIONS, INC.
Menlo Park, California

50 ONE-MINUTE TIPS FOR TRAINERS

A QUICK AND EASY GUIDE

Carrie A. Van Daele

CREDITS
Managing Editor: **Kathleen Barcos**
Editor: **Janis Paris**
Typesetting: **ExecuStaff**
Cover Design: **Carol Harris**
Artwork: **Ralph Mapson**

Copyright © 1995 by Crisp Publications, Inc.

Printed in the United States of America by Bawden Printing Company.

English language Crisp books are distributed worldwide. Our major international distributors include:

CANADA: Reid Publishing Ltd., Box 69559–109 Thomas St., Oakville, Ontario, Canada L6J 7R4. TEL: (905) 842-4428, FAX: (905) 842-9327

Raincoast Books Distribution Ltd., 112 East 3rd Avenue, Vancouver, British Columbia, Canada V5T 1C8. TEL: (604) 873-6581, FAX: (604) 874-2711

AUSTRALIA: Career Builders, P.O. Box 1051, Springwood, Brisbane, Queensland, Australia 4127. TEL: 841-1061, FAX: 841-1580

NEW ZEALAND: Career Builders, P.O. Box 571, Manurewa, Auckland, New Zealand. TEL: 266-5276, FAX: 266-4152

JAPAN: Phoenix Associates Co., Mizuho Bldg. 2-12-2, Kami Osaki, Shinagawa-Ku, Tokyo 141, Japan. TEL: 3-443-7231, FAX: 3-443-7640

Selected Crisp titles are also available in other languages. Contact International Rights Manager Suzanne Kelly at (415) 323-6100 for more information.

Library of Congress Catalog Card Number 95-68289
Van Daele, Carrie A.
50 One-Minute Tips for Trainers
ISBN 1-56052-352-2

This book is printed on recyclable paper with soy ink.

TO THE READER

This book is an important reference guide to be used frequently by trainers as an immediate and constant source of information. The information is applicable in many different training situations such as groups, one-on-one, and internal or external training sessions.

This book examines the purpose and importance of training and development programs. It discusses the 50 most important tips to consider before training your audience. You will learn about the importance of determining needs in order to know who should receive training, what skills are necessary, and at what level your audience should be taught. You will also learn about how to prepare a training manual, room arrangement, and audio-visual aids.

It is hoped you will see improved job performance from your employees as a result of your improved training skills.

In this book, you will learn about how to prepare yourself for training and how to organize and deliver your presentation to get a standing ovation from your audience.

Carrie A. Van Daele

Carrie A. Van Daele

ABOUT THIS BOOK

This book will help you effectively deliver any type of instructional material to an adult audience both on the job and in the classroom.

There are three ways this book can be used. First, it is a permanent reference guide that can be consulted at any time and in any training situation. Second, it is your personal resource, which will provide you with practical training techniques. Third, it can be used by anyone who is responsible for the development and delivery of training. This quick reference book will guide you through all the steps of effective training.

You will learn how to:

- Determine needs
- Organize your presentation
- Prepare the training manual
- Deliver your presentation
- Understand how adults learn
- Arrange the training room
- Prepare yourself for training
- Use a variety of audio-visual aids

You will also learn the following theoretical concepts:

- The principles of how adults learn
- The purpose and concept of instructional delivery techniques
- The purpose and components of a lesson plan
- Various communication skills; that is, speaking, listening, and questioning skills

ABOUT THE AUTHOR

Carrie Van Daele has an extensive business background in Organizational Development—specifically Training and Development in areas such as management, team building, selling, customer service, strategic planning for companies, and more.

Currently, Carrie is president of Van Daele & Associates Consulting, Inc., a full-service human resources consulting firm.

Carrie has provided consulting for a wide variety of industries such as manufacturers, banks, retail and service, transportation, city governments, and universities. She has conducted training seminars for over 300 companies around the United States and Canada. Carrie has also taught college-level courses for over ten years at various universities.

Carrie welcomes the opportunity to share her training experiences and knowledge with you and hopes the material in this book will benefit you for the rest of your training days.

Dedication

This book is dedicated to my husband, Terry M. Van Daele, who inspires me to accomplish my goals, and to hold on to my dreams. He has taught me by example to be kind to myself. His unending love gives me the strength to move forward even when I feel I am going nowhere!

Most of all, I dedicate this book to my daughter, Ronee A. Van Daele, who is always patient with me during my long working hours. Ronee gives me unconditional love during my ups and downs. Thank you, Ronee.

CONTENTS

CONTENTS (continued)

SECTION

1

Determine the Needs

ESTABLISH THE TIME NEEDED FOR TRAINING

Write down the objectives of your lesson. Objectives are short sentences that describe the actual knowledge or skills you need to convey.

Here are two guidelines:

1. The lesson is too long if more than four or five closely related objectives are required to describe what the training session is to include. Shorten the lesson and leave some of the material for another lesson.

2. The lesson may be too short for some participants if only one or two objectives cover the lesson.

Remember, the number of ideas/skills to be included also depends upon the general ability of the learners.

What other factors can you think of that might affect the amount of time you establish for your training session?

_____

_____

_____

_____

_____

DEFINE LEARNER OUTCOMES

These are the skills that learners should be able to demonstrate by the end of the training session. Describe how the skills will be taught, and what performance standards are required.

Specifically, what is the learning for, and what is the immediate payback to the organization and to the individual? You need to analyze the skills employees will be required to perform "on the job" (researching their job descriptions if necessary).

Measuring new skills in light of the stated objectives tells you when the training process is complete and helps ensure that the learning should last beyond the training experience.

Education is a short-term investment while development is a long-term investment. For your audience, jot down which goals are of immediate importance to the organization versus long-term.

Immediate Skills	Long-Term Goals

KEEP YOUR OBJECTIVES FRIENDLY

Objectives should be written in the second person with the subject "you" being understood—not the overly formalized third person.

► Avoid wordiness in your objectives. Introduce terms. Don't assume the learner already knows the basics. Start with the basics before moving on to advanced skills.

► Avoid crowding objectives. It is okay to have your objectives stand alone. Don't crowd too many behaviors into one long sentence.

For each of the following objectives, identify how the phrasing of each could be improved. Rewrite the objective, using the tips you have learned.

"You should be able to design and
print a letter using your new
software."

_____
_____
_____

"You will be able to change the oil,
test the plugs, and rotate the tires."

_____
_____
_____

"One will be able to transfer the
design to his or her own fabric."

_____
_____
_____

6

TIP #4   IDENTIFY THE PARTS OF YOUR OBJECTIVE

► An **action verb** describes a specific behavior or activity, as in

Example: *"Describe the six steps . . ."*

► Following the verb should be a **content reference,** as in

Example: "Describe the six steps *in the wheel-making process . . ."*

► Now add a **performance standard** to indicate minimal acceptable accomplishment in measurable terms. Your objective might read something like

Example: "Describe the six steps in the wheel-making process *in five minutes or less . . ."*

► If necessary for clarity in a specific job description, a **criteria** or **condition** should be added to the objective:

Example: "When given a set of photographs, the learner should describe the six steps in the wheel-making process *in correct order* in five minutes or less."

PUT THE OBJECTIVES IN SEQUENCE

This works well when trying to structure the objectives in a specific pattern, for instance, from the easiest to the most difficult.

The following categories of learning objectives are listed in terms of difficulty of learning comprehension. Let's look at an example. The subject matter is "Management and Leadership." After completing this course, you should be able to:

Factual Learning Objectives

These skill-oriented items of information deal with names, dates, places, events, or basic terminology related to specific subject areas. *For example:*

1. Define leadership.

2. Describe the major characteristics of the five leadership styles.

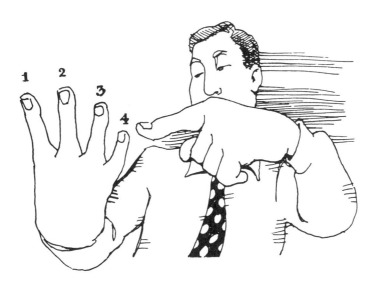

TIP #5 (continued)

Conceptual Learning Objectives

These knowledge-oriented items discriminate between objects and events by classifying or grouping those with similar characteristics under general titles or category classifications or ranks. *For example:*

> ### *List of Key Concepts to Know*
>
> | | |
> |---|---|
> | Leadership | Managerial Roles |
> | Role Behavior | Employee Involvement |
> | Autocratic Style | Corporate Style |

1. Understand the role that culture and globalization plays in leadership effectiveness.

2. Understand the complexity of the leadership process.

Principle Learning Objectives

These key-principles-to-remember items are statements showing relationships among two or more concepts.

1. Leadership is the behavior of an individual when he or she is directing the activities of a group toward a shared goal.

2. Leadership is the influential increment over and above mechanical compliance with the routine directives of the organization.

IDENTIFY TRAINING NEEDS

While reading the next tip, try to think of a training course that would remedy your organization's biggest need.

Identify Your Primary Purpose

Your primary purpose is to design and/or purchase a training program that will facilitate or strengthen the job performance of each learner.

Determine the Organization's Needs

Determine the specific performance level the organization demands for the future. It is important to match your training objectives to the organization's objectives.

Determine the Existing Performance Level

Analyze the existing performance level of the person or work group. Make sure that the information is soundly based and doesn't just represent your personal opinions.

What training course(s) would you recommend to your supervisor to improve your organization?

_____

_____

_____

_____

_____

SECTION 1: REVIEW

You have now completed Section One. Do you know how to determine training needs? Answer these questions after you have read each tip in this section.

How are your training needs directly related to the employees' job?

_____

_____

Who needs the training and why?

_____

_____

What training courses will meet the training needs and why?

_____

_____

How will training be structured to meet the business demands?

_____

_____

When will training be conducted?

_____

_____

Where will training be conducted?

_____

_____

What job performance improvements do you want to see as a result of training?

_____

_____

How will training be measured?

_____

_____

How will the employees be held accountable in order to guarantee that the training information will be practiced on the job?

_____

_____

SECTION

2

Prepare the Training Manual

WRITE AN EASY-TO-READ TRAINING MANUAL

The training manual is a step-by-step outline of what the participants will learn, what they will be able to apply to their jobs, and how to do it. The manual should contain the topic content as well as exercises and other activities, background materials, supporting charts and graphs, and room for notes. It is your reference for the course. It is also the participants' on-the-job reference upon completion of the course.

The first step in designing a training manual is to answer the following questions:

► How many manuals will be developed and for whom?

► Why do we need a manual?

► How will the manual be used?

► What needs to be written and illustrated in the manual?

► How many pages will the manual contain?

► How and by whom will the manual be produced?

► Is there a requirement for the manual to be produced using a specific medium?

► How many copies of the manual will be distributed?

► How often will the manual be updated?

► What design specification and style of binder will be used?

TIP #7 (continued)

Training Manual Contents

A training manual often contains many, if not all, of these parts:

Title Page

Management Endorsement (optional)

Table of Contents

How to Use This Manual

Body of the Manual

Appendices (if used)

Subject Index

Forms Index (if necessary)

Now, it is just a matter of getting started. First, you should gather all the available subject material.

Consult the following:

▶ Manuals that may already exist.

▶ Files from the involved department

▶ Personnel department, who will provide you with job descriptions, organizational charts, and policy documents.

▶ Systems department, who will provide you with flowcharts, diagrams, and other documentation

▶ Legal department, who will provide you with local, national, and international legislative information

Divide the Subject Material into Tabs, Sections and Subjects

TAB	SECTION	SUBJECT
1 General	**1** Introduction	**1.01** Meal Planning **1.02** Quick and easy meals
	2 The Kitchen Cupboard	**2.01** Staples **2.02** Spices **2.03** Flavors **2.04** Herbs
	3 Methods of Cooking	**3.01** Steaming **3.02** Broiling **3.03** Boiling **3.04** Deep Frying **3.05** Microwave **3.06** Crockpot

KEEP IT SIMPLE

▶ **Write for the Audience**

The content, style, language (level of difficulty), and layout must be suited to the reader's needs.

▶ **Organize Your Material**

The readers must be able to follow your meaning. The material must be organized into bits of information with headings and captions, so the reader does not have to consume large amounts of data to get a single fact.

▶ **Rewrite, Revise, and Edit Your Material**

Don't be offended when your drafts come back with many corrections and revisions. You want to achieve clarity, simplicity, continuity, and brevity.

▶ **Use Charts and Illustrations to Support Your Message**

"A picture is worth a thousand words." Break up the text with graphs, illustrations, tables, matrices, and diagrams. You want your reader to visualize your point.

▶ **Identify Your Subject**

You must know what to aim for when you begin a manual. If you don't know enough about the subject, then you must learn.

▶ **Use Clear, Short, Familiar Words**

Don't use a big word when a short one will do. The readers may become aggravated by the inconvenience of having to look up a word in the dictionary.

► Eliminate Unnecessary Words

Description words such as adjectives and adverbs are not required in manuals because they obscure the meaning.

For example, look at the first sentence and then the second sentence.

1. The coffee cup, which was sitting on the edge of the counter, suddenly fell with a loud crash.

2. The coffee cup fell.

If you only have one coffee cup, there is no need to describe where and how.

► Keep Sentences Short and Simple

An appropriate average sentence length for manuals is between 10–15 words. For example, compare the following two sentences. Which sentence is more concise and to the point?

1. It should be observed that not very many—in fact only 15—cases of absenteeism took place in the second month of this year, February, the very month, in fact, when the new system was begun.

2. Only 15 cases of absenteeism were recorded during February, the month the new system was begun.

► Use the Active Voice

The active voice emphasizes the subject. The passive voice emphasizes the verb. Let your subject *do something*, rather than have your object *be done to*.

For example, compare these two sentences for clarity.

1. Mickey Mouse *was hit* right on his little yellow head by Kay.

2. Kay (subject) *hit* Mickey Mouse right on his little yellow head.

TIP #8 (continued)

▶ **Use the Imperative Mood**

Use this in conjunction with the active voice. In the imperative mood, the second personal pronoun "you" is understood and need not be written, as in, "Open the mail."

▶ **Use Notes**

Notes are used to highlight points or to reference other information that is relevant to the text. Leave white space between them and the rest of the text.

▶ **Use Emphasis**

Underlining, italics, or boldface can be used to emphasize a point. Keep it to a minimum, once or twice a page, if necessary.

▶ **Use Ordering Techniques**

Here is a simple outline, using Arabic numerals, then lowercase letters. If more levels are needed, you can use Roman numerals and capital letters in addition to those shown here (for example: I., A., 1., a.).

```
1.

2.

        a.

        b.

3.

4.
```

▶ **Use Point Form**

When listing three or more items, use point form. Use numbers or letters for sequential items, and dashes or bullets for nonsequential lists.

To show hierarchy in lists, use bullets for primary topic and dashes for secondary topics. For example:

- Good foods to eat

  – vegetables

  – fruit

- Bad foods to eat

  – candy

  – cakes

► **Avoid Using Only Male Pronouns**

Try to avoid the use of male pronouns to include "all" people. Use the his or her approach to writing. Use "he" in certain illustrations, "she" in others. With a little effort you can rephrase sentences so that you don't even need a possessive pronoun. Or simply make the subject plural.

1. Notify the employee on the first day of his or her six-month probationary term.

2. Notify the employee on the first day of the six-month probationary term.

3. Notify employees on the first day of the six-month probationary term.

SECTION 2: CHECKLIST

You have now completed Section Two. Use this checklist to identify the tasks for which you will be responsible. Check those you feel you must gain more knowledge about.

- ☐ Gather material
- ☐ Create a table of contents
- ☐ Set up a schedule
- ☐ Investigate and choose a medium, e.g., computer
- ☐ Design a title page
- ☐ Order the binders, tab dividers, and paper
- ☐ Write the material (first draft)
- ☐ Procure illustrations
- ☐ Translate material to computer
- ☐ Proofread and correct the first draft
- ☐ Obtain critique of the first draft
- ☐ Rework material as necessary
- ☐ Obtain approvals
- ☐ Produce illustrations
- ☐ Prepare indexes
- ☐ Arrange printing, collating, and punching
- ☐ Set up distribution system
- ☐ Schedule periodic reviews
- ☐ Schedule user education

SECTION

3

Understand How Adults Learn

CONSIDER THE BASICS

Even before you begin to plan the learning experiences it is well to consider a few basic facts. Apply these basic concepts to your adult learners.

▶ *We learn best when we are ready to learn.* When we have a strong purpose, a well-fixed reason for learning, it is easier to receive instruction and to make progress.

▶ *We develop skill through practice.* The more often we use what we have learned, the better we can perform or understand it. Use it or lose it!

▶ *We learn faster when the results are satisfying to us.* If what we have learned is useful and beneficial, we are more likely to want to learn more.

▶ *We tie learning to what we already know.* Learning something new is made easier if the learning can be built upon what we already know. It is best to start with simple steps that are related to what we can now do (or already understand) and then proceed to new and more difficult tasks or ideas.

▶ *We learn one thing at a time.* Learning has to be accomplished step-by-step. Thus, learning proceeds in an orderly way, one step at a time.

▶ *We learn by doing.* Learning becomes complete when we put into practice what we are attempting to learn.

▶ *Successful learning stimulates more learning.* Failure to learn or to understand discourages further learning. You need to plan instruction so that successful learning is assured at each step of the way.

▶ *We get new impressions through our five senses.* The five senses are: seeing, hearing, feeling, tasting, and smelling. It is through the sense of sight that the greater part of learning occurs. The sources of the sight are observable actions, pictures, and written material. Since so much of learning begins with what the learner sees, the trainer must make every effort to use this medium effectively.

▶ *We learn differently.* We differ from one another in experiences, abilities, and background, and we learn at different rates. In addition to the general principles of adult learning, adults also bring unique characteristics to the course or seminar.

UNDERSTAND ADULT LEARNERS' DIFFERENCES

Ways and means of teaching are known as *teaching methods.* You will not know which methods to select or how to use them unless you first understand how adult learners comprehend information.

- Adults' peak of learning ability is reached between 20 and 25 years.

- Adults are less likely to accept external motivation. They want to know the "why."

- Adults are serious learners once motivated.

- Adults are more interested in problem solving than information gathering. Therefore, use job-related case studies and simulated exercises.

- Adults vary greatly in education and past experience.

- Adults may have to "unlearn" first.

- Adults want feedback on how they are doing.

REVIEW YOUR TEACHING METHODS

While reading the following review of learning principles, keep in mind areas in which you would like to improve.

Learning Progresses Best Step-By-Step

- Cover one major point at a time.
- Move in small progressive steps from known to unknown, from simple to complex.
- Build learner's confidence.

Learning Is Stimulated By Response Or Participation

- Participation strengthens learning experience.
- It converts learning from passive to active experience.
- It develops patterns of behavior essential to learning skills.
- It generates and maintains learner interest.

Learning Is Speeded By Visualization

- Visualization increases impact on the mind by employing multiple sensory impressions.
- It converts abstract ideas and concepts into concrete, easier-to-understand form.
- It increases retention and recall—up to five times over methods not employing visualization.

TIP #11 (continued)

Learning Is Maintained By Recency and Use

- People remember best and use most effectively what they've learned most recently.

- People seldom learn an idea or action by hearing about it or doing it once.

- Learning regresses or deteriorates when not put to use.

- The new skill should be put to use as soon as possible and practiced often for maximum learning.

Learning Is Stimulated By Results and Rewards

- Students need to know the reason or purpose of the learning.

- A reinforcing learning experience satisfies the desire for recognition and approval.

- A motivated learner desires to achieve and excel through continued learning and desire to improve.

Areas that I would like to emphasize in my training style:

_____

_____

_____

_____

_____

_____

DEAL WITH FRUSTRATED LEARNERS

What happens when an individual encounters frustration in the training situation? Psychologists tell us that frustration occurs in an individual when a need is not satisfied. In the learning situation, the trainee has the need to learn but for some reason—either internal or external—he or she does not learn as he or she would like to. When a need is stifled or not satisfied, the learner can very often display frustrated behavior, which you may misinterpret. These mechanisms of frustration can fit into one of the following categories:

Aggression → The student may seem bored, disruptive, argumentative, or want to fight.

Projection → Here the learner finds something or someone else to blame when he/she isn't doing well.

Flight → The learner escapes from frustration by day-dreaming or missing class.

Rationalization → Here the learner finds what he/she thinks is a good reason or explanation for not doing something.

Resignation → Or the student may simply give up.

If the behavior of your learners indicates frustration, you should examine the learning situation. Remember that although you are not a trained psychologist, you must attempt to determine the underlying cause for learner frustration. If possible, try to correct the source of frustration.

SEE TIP #13 FOR COPING TECHNIQUES

EXERCISE: *Working Through Negative Behavior*

For practice, try to identify the underlying frustration that might be the cause of each behavior. What might you do to remedy it?

Behavior	Symptom	Remedy
Aggression	Argumentative	_____
	Sabotage	_____
	Disruption	_____
	Apathy	_____
Dissatisfaction	Low Morale	_____
	Carelessness	_____
	Absenteeism	_____
	Excessive Breaks	_____
	Tardiness	_____

LEARN COPING TECHNIQUES

1. Don't take frustrated learners personally.

2. Pause and think out your strategy. Write out your script about what you need to say to the frustrated learner. Use the following formula.

   • Identify the problem. Mention only facts about what you see, hear, feel, taste, and/or smell.

   • Describe some possible causes without placing blame on the person.

3. Use reflective statements about facts or inferences (assumptions). Describe your statements as either a fact or personal opinion. Try not to make your personal opinion sound judgmental. Learn to use an "I feel . . ." statement, and then follow up by asking the frustrated learner to confirm your assumption about what is happening to him or her.

4. Examine your teaching style. "Do I need to vary my teaching style in this situation?"

5. Ask for feedback. Ask the frustrated learner to brainstorm about possible solutions.

6. Continue or redirect the learner to another resource. You might reach a point where you cannot help the learner. At this point, you will need to discuss any action with the learner's immediate supervisor and/or human resources department.

HANDLE PROBLEM PARTICIPANTS

Following are some problem personality "types" and some suggestions about how to deal with each.

The Disinterested Type

- Stress personal benefits to be gained from the training.

- Direct questions at this individual to get involvement.

- Seat this person in the middle of discussion flow.

The Argumentative Type

- Direct questions raised by others back to this individual for answering.

- Direct this person's questions to the group for answering.

- Avoid being drawn into an argument—let the group settle issues.

- Seat this person at your immediate right or left.

The Overly Talkative Type

- Direct questions away from this individual to other members of the group.

- Talk to this individual privately and suggest the value of letting others participate.

- Seat this person on your immediate right or left.

The Rambling Type

- Suggest listing the points presented to lead these individuals into organizing ideas.

- Briefly summarize all important points so far, to bring them into focus.

- Point out the need to stay on schedule to curtail rambling.

The Controversial Type

- Try to foresee points of controversy and plan answers to them.

- Defer points for later report.

- Defer points for private discussion.

SECTION 3: SELF-TEST

You have now completed Section Three. As a skills check, fill in the blank spaces of the following items.

1. Adults are more problem than information centered. Therefore, use

   _____ case studies and _____ exercises.

2. We develop _____ through practice.

3. We _____ differently.

4. Learning is maintained by _____ and _____ .

5. Learning is speeded by _____ .

6. Learning is stimulated by response or _____ .

7. Learning progresses best _____ .

8. Identify the problem. Mention only facts about what you _____ .

9. _____ some possible causes of frustration without placing blame.

10. Try to foresee points of _____ and plan answers to them.

SECTION

4

Prepare Yourself
for Training

EXAMINE YOUR ATTITUDES

In the previous sections, you had an opportunity to challenge any popular misconceptions about training that you might have held. Take the following self-test to see if your attitudes have changed.

What do you feel?	Yes	Not Sure	No
Do you feel that "trial and error" is the best teacher?	☐	☐	☐
Do you feel that training is a job that should be handled by specialists since you don't have time for it?	☐	☐	☐
Do you feel that meetings can only be a waste of time?	☐	☐	☐
Do you feel that once you've told someone how to do a given job that he or she should be able to do it?	☐	☐	☐
Do you feel that there is one best way to impart information to others?	☐	☐	☐

Check Yourself: Any *Yes* or *Not Sure* answers indicate a need to reexamine your attitudes.

USE A LESSON PLAN

The lesson plan is a blueprint for instruction and will help assure that all essential lesson contents are included in a logical, sequential, well-organized manner. These lesson plan components are listed here:

► A Title

The lesson title should be behaviorally descriptive, yet concise. For instance, *Learn How to Be More Assertive on the Job.*

► Learner Outcomes

Learner outcomes are the changes in job behavior you wish to accomplish. Refer to them frequently. Keep the outcomes in front of you as you plan and teach.

► Instructional Aids and Materials

Include tools, equipment, handouts, overhead, films—in short, all aids or materials essential for instruction. Prior to the lesson make sure these tools are available and ready for use.

► Content Outline

Outline the skills or information to be presented in the lesson. The outline should present the main points logically (in sequence and in ascending order of content difficulty). The content should also contain subtopics you wish the students to retain.

► Instructional Reminders

Instructional reminders are specific details you wish to incorporate as the training session progresses; for instance, time limits, personal anecdotes, specific questions, notations about training aids, and so on.

► Review

The review may consist of oral questions or actual task performances.

PRACTICE MAKES PROFESSIONAL

Because the trainer is performing in front of an audience, the trainer must look professional. The voice and the body are the primary instructional tools used in this situation. In addition, trainers recognize the need for effective visual aids and know they must be able to use them well. The act of coordinating audio-visual material and equipment with the verbal act of instructing is difficult and challenging. Rehearsal, training experience, patience, and looking at other professional trainers in action is part of the growth and development process with instructional speaking skills.

In addition, listening is another critical communication skill that trainers must use constantly and at a very proficient level. Listening with the eyes is as essential as listening with the ears. Trainers must watch the expression on learners' faces, the body posture shown in the class, and other nonverbal signals that express attitudes.

IMPROVE YOUR VOICE

There are specific categories of instructional speaking skills. For a more professional presentation, you can break down the various vocal techniques into areas that you can work on individually:

Pitch

Use a comfortable and pleasant sounding pitch (the highness or lowness of your voice) that will not tax the voice of the instructor or the ears of the trainees.

Volume

The loudness and softness of the voice must vary from location to location as well as take into account the numbers in attendance.

Speech Rate

The rate of speaking must vary depending on the difficulty and significance of material, and whether notetaking is expected of the trainees. Present difficult material at a slower speed than easy material. Also, pause frequently to give the participants a chance to comprehend the materials. (Plan the material so you know it fits within your timeframe.)

Pacing and Pausing

Silence can be as emphatic as your voice. It can mark the shift from one activity to another. Research indicates that pausing also affects communication in the following ways:

- Silence helps the learner to process information.
- You can use it to get attention.
- You can use it to emphasize a point.

Vocal Inflection

The tonal ranges of the voice display excitement and energy or lack of it. This display also indicates the importance of information and provides personal commentary. Strive for vocal variety by varying the volume of your voice, especially taking into consideration the size of the class, room size, room arrangement, and other physical conditions.

Articulation

If words are mispronounced, you will be misunderstood. Practice pronouncing difficult words prior to class. Use caution when pronouncing uncommon words; write the unknown words on the board or easel. Do not slur or run words together by speaking too rapidly. And look at your audience when speaking to them.

Projection

The power behind the flow of vocal air is critical. The sounds of the voice must travel to every set of ears in attendance—without tiring or damaging the instructor's voice with simple laryngitis or major vocal injury. Trainers need strong voices that can operate for long periods of time, day after day. Try to stay relaxed while breathing so that your breathing is not shallow (use your whole chest, not just the upper portion, for air support).

Helpful Hints for Better Voice Control

Keep a copy of this exercise where you can practice it frequently.

1. Open your mouth wide whenever speaking.

2. Use yawning and smiling as a warm up exercise.

3. Rinse out your mouth prior to speaking at worksite.

4. An excellent phrase exercise is "red leather, yellow leather."

5. Stress the last syllable of a word or phrase to improve diction.

6. Don't drop word endings; for example, *ing; ed, s, th, d,* and *ng.*

7. Distinguish clearly between: "t" and "d", and "p" and "b", "f" and "v", and "m" and "n."

8. Inhale through the nose in quick but deep breaths, using total lung capacity.

9. Exhale through the mouth in a controlled and much slower fashion.

USE EYE CONTACT

Using your eyes to measure the comprehension of your listeners is critical. But you may also use your eyes to question, praise, encourage, challenge, assess, select, and rebuke. It is the most efficient feedback tool available to the trainer.

Remember to:

- ✔ Look at your audience.
- ✔ Distribute your eye contact evenly over the entire audience.
- ✔ Shift your gaze smoothly from one segment of the audience to another.

BECOME BODY AWARE

Body stance and posture are on display when the instructor is in front of a class. A more significant fact is the amount of time a trainer must be on her or his feet, making it essential that the skeletal framework be able to support the body weight for long periods of time. Body posture also presents a wide variety of nonverbal messages in a class.

Your motion gets the participants' attention. Your body movements should be natural, not too jerky. Your physical movement from one side of the room to another keeps the participant attention directly on you during your presentation.

Using your arms and hands helps visually support the knowledge and skills presented in training classes. These movements also help to place information into series—as well as demonstrate what information takes priority. A shrug of your shoulders, a glance at the ceiling, or crossing your arms may convey more meaning than words. Using your hands and arms to point or clap as well as raising your eyebrows, smiling, or even frowning can be used to direct the participants' attention to a thought, concept, or skill.

Mannerisms to Avoid

Here are examples of behaviors that distract learners from what you are saying. Place a ✔ by each behavior you know you have done.

- ☐ Rattling pocket coins
- ☐ Repeating expressions such as "you know," or "okay"
- ☐ Leaning over the lectern
- ☐ Tossing a piece of chalk in the air or playing with pencil
- ☐ Pacing back and forth in the same location
- ☐ Hands and arms clasped in front of body (fig leaf position) or behind back (parade rest position)
- ☐ Scratching
- ☐ Playing with hair or constantly brushing it away from face
- ☐ Rubbing hands together
- ☐ Twisting ring or jewelry

Helpful Hints for Better Body Control

Try out some of these tips in front of a mirror until they feel natural.

1. Exercise and keep your body healthy so that you have the stamina for a training session.
2. Balance body weight equally on both feet when standing for a long time period.
3. Move about the room to avoid favoring one side.
4. Sit on the edge of the instructor table or desk when trainees have the focus of attention to get a "rest break" for the body and to convey a sense of relaxed, frank discussion.
5. When not using arms and hands let them hang at your side for a rest.
6. Avoid orchestrating with pens, rulers, and the like when gesturing since these can look visually threatening.

PROJECT CREDIBILITY

Sincerity: This is one vital quality all trainers must display at all times. This stimulates motivation and enhances the learning process. It is the basis for display of professionalism.

Self-Confidence: Trainers must role model this quality to get the type of positive cooperation necessary for learning to flourish. This is the basis of credibility. Trainers must exhibit credibility from the very beginning of the training encounter. Trainer credibility correlates very highly with the productivity of training programs.

Rapport: The psychological relationship developed between the trainer and the trainees must be a positive one. The quality and effectiveness of this relationship influences credibility, sincerity, motivation, and self-confidence. This relationship also affects the attitudes and job behaviors trainees take back to their work environment.

Developing Rapport

Here are two suggestions for developing a sincere and friendly atmosphere. For your training situation, can you come up with any others?

► Use morning coffee opener, breaks, lunches, or related evening meals as valuable time to interpersonalize and develop positive attitudes that will carry back into the training class.

► Be generous with praise and recognize contributions. Use responses to trainee questions or requests for information as a means for giving compliments.

► Other:

_____

_____

_____

THINK BEFORE YOU SPEAK—VOCABULARY

Before you can express an idea clearly, all relevant terms must first be thoroughly understood. Some rules to remember include the following:

1. Use a common vocabulary.

2. Consider the educational level of the participants.

3. Define technical terms.

4. Do not assume acronyms are understood by the participants.

5. Use short sentences as a way to emphasize points.

6. Eliminate unnecessary words and phrases in your presentation.

7. Be specific, not vague.

What are the 10 or so terms most likely to be misunderstood in your field? (List acronyms and jargon as well as any objects or actions that are referred to by more than one term.)

_____

_____

_____

_____

_____

_____

ASK QUESTIONS

For the learner, questions provide many opportunities to enhance their experience.

Questions:

- Provide the opportunity to get detailed or more clarified information.

- Permit interaction that facilitates the learning process.

- Allow for individualized attention when it is needed.

- Permit the trainee to share learning experiences with peers and trainer.

You can develop your technique of asking questions, to encourage the maximum trainee response. Follow these rules:

RULE #1   Address the question in a clearly decided direction—a trainee or the entire class.

RULE #2   Phrase the question as concisely (and briefly) as possible.

RULE #3   Know at least one adequate response prior to stating the question before the group.

RULE #4   Allow a moment of thought, especially if the question is long, difficult, or contains more than one point.

RULE #5   Once the response has been given, always provide an assessment and a positive remark.

RESPOND TO QUESTIONS

There are certain steps to follow when responding to a question in a training session—producing an atmosphere of respect and interaction.

(Listen)

Listen objectively and completely to the question without interruption. Avoid letting bias block out part of the question. Avoid making judgments about the trainee asking the question.

(Repeat)

Direct the question back to the entire class. Make certain all can hear it and involve the class in the discussion. Use this time for mental analysis of the question and to get the complete attention of the total group.

(Respond)

Respond truthfully and briefly as possible. Relate the response to the instructional material or the learning objectives whenever possible. Use a visual aid such as the blackboard or flipchart if it will clarify or simplify the response. Don't make up answers if you don't know. If the answer is not known, respond accordingly: "I don't have the information with me, but I can get it to you"; "I don't know off-hand, but I can tell you where to look for the information"; "I am not certain of the answer, but can someone else help me with any information?"

48

TIP #23 (continued)

What to Do When You Can't Answer

There are often situations where learners will ask questions whose answers are not in your lesson plan or notes. Read the following situations and corresponding techniques. See if you can write an example question for each situation.

Situation	Proper Technique	Question
Information within scope of course	Offer to find out. Keep the promise. Relate information to class.	_____
Material of interest only to advanced students	Identify sources of information. Help students find it. Describe process to find out.	_____
No exact information available	Inform participants that facts are not known. This might make for a good open discussion.	_____
Unrelated to topic being studied	Indicate question is outside scope of class. Offer to help find information.	_____

PREPARE THIS TEN-STEP CHECKLIST

Place a checkmark in the box for each item you have the answer to. Research and prepare in any remaining areas before making your presentation.

STEP 1: Know Your Audience

☐ How large will your audience be?

☐ What is the age, gender, and educational range of your audience?

☐ Why does this group meet? What common interests bring the members together?

☐ What other characteristics typify this audience?

STEP 2: Know the Reason for Training

☐ What is the nature of the individual or group to be trained?

☐ What problems have created the need for training?

☐ What needs to be achieved as a result of the training?

STEP 3: Know the Occasion

☐ Is the occasion solemn, formal, or casual?

☐ Does the audience hope to be informed, entertained, or inspired? Or all three?

☐ What is the timeframe?

TIP #25 (continued)

STEP 4: Know Your Speaking Environment

☐ How large a room will you be in?

☐ How will the room be arranged?

STEP 5: Customize Your Topic to Fit the Audience

☐ Why did the group ask you to speak?

☐ What information do you have that would provide most benefit to group members?

☐ How can you adapt your special knowledge so that it will both fulfill the expectations of the audience and appeal to their special interests?

STEP 6: Begin Developing Your Presentation

☐ Have you included stories, examples, illustrations, and factual evidence?

☐ Have you included illustrations from your personal experience?

☐ Have you developed more ideas than you will actually need for your speech?

☐ Have you gathered the facts and statistics?

☐ Have you gathered quotes or testimonials?

Step 7: Prepare Your Introduction to the Presentation

☐ Is your introduction dramatic, humorous, or unusual enough?

☐ Does your introduction conclude with a clear and simple statement of your point of view?

☐ Is your language clear and vivid enough to assure that your speech will be well-organized and your audience will be well entertained?

STEP 8: Critique Your Discussion

☐ Does your discussion provide evidence for your audience to agree or disagree with your point of view?

☐ Does your discussion concentrate on developing a few points clearly and precisely?

☐ Have you organized your discussion so that your points logically flow?

☐ Have you collected anecdotes, stories, humorous references, or illustrations—enough to illustrate the meaning of your facts and statistics?

STEP 9: In Conclusion

☐ How will you cue your audience that your conclusion is forthcoming?

☐ How will you summarize the most important points of your presentation?

☐ Will you clearly and explicitly state exactly what action you would like your listeners to take?

☐ Will you leave them with a memory of you and your speech? (You should!)

STEP 10: Follow Up

☐ Have you determined mechanisms by which you will obtain feedback on your presentation?

☐ Have you determined if follow up is necessary, and if so how it will be undertaken?

52

PRESENT FROM YOUR NOTES

Do not read your manuscript; instead you must transfer your material to "memory joggers." You should include one word, short phrase, symbol, or letter to remind you of each section of your speech. Avoid the temptation to include sentences or whole segments of your speech. Personally type or handwrite your notes. Use an outline format to organize your notes, with each item (and page or note card) clearly numbered. Write out all numbers or quotes that need to be cited exactly.

PRACTICE, PRACTICE, PRACTICE

Rank the following suggestions in the order that you think doing the exercise would improve your performance.

_____ Have you practiced varying your eye contact among four or five locations distributed throughout the room, holding your eye contact for several seconds at each location?

_____ Have you exaggerated variations in the pitch, rate, and volume of your speaking during practice sessions?

_____ Have you exaggerated gestures? You should, especially if you are shy.

_____ Have you recorded yourself on video or audio?

_____ Have you practiced to the point that your notes are almost unnecessary?

CONTROL YOUR NERVOUSNESS

To manage your nervousness, imagine your audience responding exactly as you want them to: eager, laughing, applauding, requesting more information, asking questions, thanking you, etc.

Accept the fact that you may have nervous symptoms on the day of your presentation. It may help to recall instances when you were nervous but went on to the more important business of sharing your knowledge and enthusiasm with your audience.

List any techniques you may have used in the past or have heard about to ease feelings of nervousness.

_____

_____

_____

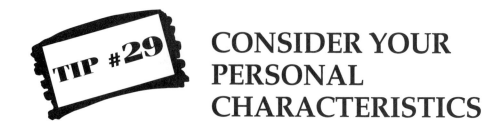

CONSIDER YOUR PERSONAL CHARACTERISTICS

Your personal characteristics determine the way you are perceived by your training participants. Your psychological and emotional characteristics influence instructional effectiveness more directly than your height, weight, color, or sex.

Attitude is important. Your feelings toward the participants and the learning process have a direct impact on the participants' interest in the course. Some participants might think, "I believe I can because you believe I can" or "I kept trying until I did it because you convinced me that I could do it."

A positive attitude also includes being creative. You must think of ways to describe or illustrate subject matter so that it comes alive for the participant. Poor instructors use the same method of presentation regardless of the topic.

Name a few of the characteristics that first come to mind when you think of your overall style:

_____

_____

_____

_____

_____

_____

APPLY CHARACTERISTICS OF EFFECTIVE TRAINERS

Following are some of the characteristics deemed most important in effective trainers.

Consideration

Instructors should be cautious in situations that may be embarrassing. Such issues as politics, racial and cultural differences, or religion are best avoided or approached with great consideration for the audience's feelings.

Cooperation

It is essential for instructors to cooperate as they work together for the benefit of participants.

Interest

You should show interest in a participant's learning and accomplishment.

Friendliness

The age-old advice to a new teacher often is "be fair, be firm, and be friendly." Positive rapport is accomplished with a smile, an exchange of greeting, and acknowledgment of another's worth.

Involvement

Behavioral and mental participation in outside recreational or social activities better acquaints the instructor with employees and managers.

TIP #30 (continued)

> ### *Don't Be Negative*
>
> You may accidently establish a reputation for being tough in a negative way by any one of the following methods:
>
> - Using aggressive behavior
> - Speaking in a commanding tone of voice
> - Frowning constantly
> - Displaying an inflexible attitude
> - Bragging or threatening
> - Refusing to repeat instructions or questions

Professionalism

You must look sharp, feel sharp, and be sharp. A clean, neat appearance is critical in any job—but a trainer is especially in a position to be observed.

Respect

If you must reprimand, do so softly. If you apply "pressure," you are more likely to arouse resistance than compliance. When a reprimand is necessary, the effective trainer:

- Remains calm
- Considers the feelings of the participant
- Discusses the matter with the student alone
- Knows and uses the facts
- Criticizes the mistake or behavior, not the person
- Includes encouragement and praise for work well done
- Suggests a constructive course of action, and
- Ends the conversation on a positive note by acknowledging the participant's past achievements and positive attributes.

SECTION 4: WORD SEARCH

The following word jumble contains 22 words trainers need to be mindful of. The words are upside down, right-side up, diagonal, and backward. Can you find all of the hidden words? The answers are in the back of the book on page 96.

```
R R P A Q G W E I V E R
L P L Z U I I R E L A X
I A A M E X D E A E J T
S A N Y S U L O H N L C
T D F O T B E N J O X E
E L L A I I L O O I S L
N C L D O S W K P T L E
E R E C N I S Q U C E S
E R S A A M E E L U S F
C L A S S C L A F D A A
N N E Y H K R W E O O C
A G A I C U I S P R R E
T H I N T H U L I T E P
S A S A I A H U L N O O
A U N B P R A C T I C E
```

Key Words:

CLASS	NATURAL	QUESTION
CREDIBLE	NOTE	RELAX
EASEL	PAUSE	REVIEW
FACE	PITCH	SELECT
HEAR	PLAN	SINCERE
INTRODUCTION	PRACTICE	SKILL
LISTEN	PROFESSIONAL	STANCE
LOOK		

SECTION

5

Organize Your
Presentation

PLAN YOUR INTRODUCTION

Here are some ideas:

► Make a shocking statement.

► Ask one or more direct questions requiring visible audience response: "Who can name some factors to consider in deciding which brand of car to buy?"

► Ask one or more rhetorical questions. These are thought-provoking questions you do not actually expect the listener to answer: "Did you ever get so fed up at work that you wanted to tell your boss off?

► Quote a well-known person or authority.

► Tell an appropriate joke.

► Present a story or an anecdote.

► Refer to the occasion, or present a hypothetical situation.

► Relate a personal experience or make a self-disclosure.

► Refer to the problem at hand, emphasizing its significance for all listeners. You can also announce your main point.

► Use a prop, visual aid, or demonstration.

PLAN THE BODY OF YOUR PRESENTATION

Here are some ideas to flush out and organize ideas in the body of your presentation. Use the *ESCAPE*[1] formula as a checklist:

ESCAPE Formula

E = **Examine** the assignment:

- What does my boss want me to do in my talk?
- What does the program chairperson or conference leader expect me to accomplish in my presentation?
- What do I want to accomplish with my listeners?
- What do my listeners want to gain from hearing my talk?
- How much time will I have to speak?

S = **State** the purpose:

- Answer the basic question: What are you going to talk about?
- What content must you develop to fulfill these expectations?

C = **Choose** ideas:

- Brainstorm
- Reference primary or secondary resources

A = **Arrange** ideas:

- Put ideas in logical arrangement
- Discriminate between the main ideas and subideas

P = **Pick** support materials:

- Develop verbal arguments
- Find audio-visuals as necessary

E = **Enhance** your presentation

- Choose presentation techniques, verbal and visual
- Practice as necessary

---

1. Adapted from Kenneth R. Mayer, *Well Spoken*.

CHOOSE AN ORDERING SYSTEM

When you write your presentation, you must choose an organizational pattern. There are several alternatives, depending upon the nature of your material:

Chronological

This is the story-telling or time-sequence approach; the speaker selects a point in time and moves forward (for instance, "history of the Mayan peoples").

Categorical

This is used when the data can be grouped into categories by common characteristics ("databases vs. spreadsheets").

Order of Importance

Here you look for priorities or qualitative differences in the information for presentation. Establish a "first, second, third, and so on" ("prime duties of law enforcement officers").

Topical

Information can also be presented topic by topic ("edible plants of the region").

Spatial

With this method content is organized around locational relationships, where objects are—up, down; left, right; east, west; Ohio; New York; and so on.

PLAN THE CLOSING OF YOUR PRESENTATION

Here are some ideas about how to end your presentation. You will usually summarize main points and often draw conclusions from facts presented in the presentation. But you may also:

1. Make recommendations.

2. Call for action or challenge the audience to act.

3. Relate an illustrative and clarifying story, anecdote, or personal application.

4. Tell an appropriate joke.

5. Use a quotation

6. Make a prediction or forecast.

7. Use a prop, visual aid, or demonstration to emphasize the major point.

HOW NOT TO PLAN

SECTION 5: THOUGHT-PROVOKING QUESTIONS

You have now completed Section Five. Take time to analyze the parts of your training package.

How have you planned your introduction?

Comment: _____

_____

_____

_____

_____

How have you planned the body of your presentation?

Comment: _____

_____

_____

_____

_____

How have you planned the closing of your presentation?

Comment: _____

_____

_____

_____

_____

SECTION

6

Deliver Your Presentation

PUT THE TRAINEE AT EASE

Put the Trainee at Ease

► Do not overwhelm the trainee with your expertise.

► Greet trainees in a friendly manner.

► Stimulate interest by explaining the advantages of being able to perform the skill or understand the new concepts.

► Stress the importance of the new skill but try to remove fears about learning the material.

Find Out What the Trainee Already Knows

► Talk to the trainee about experience related to the new skill or information (this will tell you where to start and how much to teach).

► Show the trainee how the new skill or information is related to the job or the whole operation.

OBSERVE AND FOLLOW UP

OBSERVE TRAINEES' PROGRESS

In presenting the operation you will tell and show the trainee what he or she should know and be able to do:

- Position yourself so the trainee can see all your motions.

- Explain carefully as you demonstrate each step.

- Find out if the trainee understands by asking specific questions (encourage him/her to ask questions).

- Check at the end of each step by asking the trainee to explain key concepts or to perform the task.

- Explain all new, unfamiliar, or special terms.

- Use comparisons to relate new tasks to previous experience.

- Continue until the trainee can perform the new skill by him- or herself (be helpful and take enough time with each trainee).

FOLLOW UP AS NECESSARY

Checking frequently and encouraging questions:

- Shows the trainee that you are interested in his or her success.

- Helps you determine the effectiveness of your training.

- Gives the trainee a chance to clear up any questions.

Taper off extra coaching and eliminate close follow up as the trainee masters the new skill or information. Before putting the trainee on his/her own, tell the trainee where to get help when necessary.

USE "SHOW AND TELL"

When possible, "show" as well as "tell" the new skill being taught.

Benefits include:

► Setting performance standards and policies to direct performance

► Imparting basic knowledge and information needed to perform

► Requiring limited time

► Adding tangibility to the learning experience

► Providing an experience model

► Requiring a minimum of a manager's time

	How to Apply	**Uses**
TELLING	*Lecture*	*Inform*
	Visuals:	Present and Explain
	• Flipchart	
	• Wall charts	Set Stage
	• Overhead	
	• Transparencies	Review and Sum up
	• Slides	
	• Video Tape	
	• Exhibits	
SHOWING	*Personal*	*Set Standard*
	• Demonstration	Visualize
	• Audio/Video	Performance
	• Recordings	Show Feasibility
		Reinforce and Clarify

TIP #39 INVOLVE THE PARTICIPANTS

Your role is to involve participants in an effective and constructive manner. Discussion accomplishes this and is considered to be a valuable teaching technique. Here are a few suggestions to follow:

1. Set the stage. Make sure your participants understand what is to be learned and explain the training method you plan to use.

2. Let them know their involvement is encouraged.

3. Be prepared to ask a variety of questions during discussion. Give credit where needed, tactfully clarify meaning, and suggest a review of what has been said. Ask questions of individuals to get them involved in the discussion. Draw points of view from all participants.

4. Listen. The trainer's job is to draw out the thoughts and feelings of individuals in the group. Do not become emotionally involved in the discussion.

5. Summarize the discussion (or ask trainees to do so). Clear up misconceptions.

PLAY GAMES

Games are great ice-breakers, class warm-ups and tension relievers. They are excellent for involving total class participation because they include verbal, non-verbal and physical behavior.

Games, especially those that employ role playing, can make wonderful illustrations of theories or modeling behaviors. They can also renew mental and physical energies in long sessions and can serve as session closures for summarizing theme issues.

Use of games* includes:

▶ *Getting Acquainted Exercises:* relieves tension and breaks the ice

▶ *Making Nonverbal Introductions:* encourages participation and promotes awareness of nonverbal behaviors

▶ *Following Oral Instructions:* models behavior and makes illustrations

▶ *Building Memory Activity:* renews energies

▶ *Writing Contract with Oneself:* provides closure with training and helps track long-term progress

---

*A useful reference on this subject is *Games Trainers Play* by John W. Newstrom and Edward E. Scannell. McGraw-Hill, 1980.

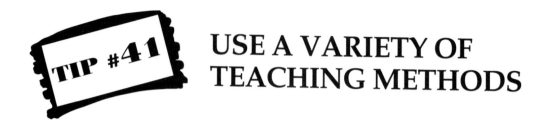

USE A VARIETY OF TEACHING METHODS

Here is a list of other techniques that can be used to add variety to the training situation:

The assignment   The trainer gives the trainee a specific work assignment to do.

The field trip   The group actually visits and sees a certain operation, procedure, setup, or process.

The laboratory   The trainees actually research a topic under laboratory conditions.

A symposium   This is perhaps the oldest training method on record. (*Webster's* defines this as "a meeting at which several speakers deliver short addresses on a topic or on related topics.")

A clinic   This is a meeting in which attendees discuss common problems and seek solutions.

Closed Circuit T.V.   Initial outlay is expensive; however, results are very good with proper use of this equipment as a training device. This method is often helpful in training:

- Sales
- Interviewing
- Appraisal
- Service
- Management

SECTION 6: RATE YOURSELF

You have just completed Section Six. Now, take some time to plan how you will implement what you have learned.

1. How do you plan to remove fears about learning the material?

_____

_____

2. How will you ensure that you greet in a friendly manner?

_____

_____

3. In what ways will you stimulate interest?

_____

_____

4. How will you find out what the trainee already knows?

_____

_____

5. Where will you position yourself for clear instruction?

_____

_____

6. How will you "show and tell" the trainee what he/she should know?

_____

_____

7. How will you practice explaining carefully as you demonstrate?

_____

_____

SECTION 6: RATE YOURSELF (continued)

8. What key points will you have the trainee explain?

_____

_____

9. How are you planning to take time with each trainee?

_____

_____

10. How will you put the trainee on his/her own yet arrange to check progress frequently?

_____

_____

S E C T I O N

7

Arrange the Room

MAKE THE ROOM ARRANGEMENT LEARNER FRIENDLY

The training room needs to be comfortable, accommodating, and afford some amount of shielding from outside distractions. This is not always possible when the training must occur on the worksite. Furnishings should be verified *prior to* your presentation:

► Chairs and tables should be comfortable.

► Tables or desks should be lightweight and movable. In fact, all furniture and equipment should be lightweight enough for quick and easy moving, or if heavy, on rollers.

► Blackboards, projection screen, podium, easel with flipcharts, overhead projector, and extension cord should be standard media equipment at every training site, although you may have to reserve them.

> **Possible Physical Arrangements**

1. Classroom/Standard

- Traditional set-up

- Operates with most audio/visual equipment

- Trainees can see trainer and all projected media displays

- Works well with tablemate-sharing activities

- Accommodates testing procedures for writing and/or viewing visual media

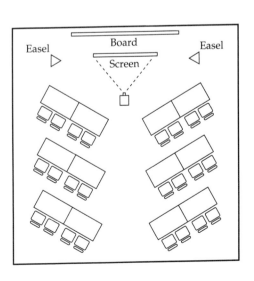

TIP #42 (continued)

2. Roundtable

- Ideal set-up for brainstorming activity

- Accommodates problem-solving activities

- Encourages informal dialogue and active listening

- Can eliminate need for a formal leader and make all trainees feel equal regardless of organizational position

- *Not* good for media projections or tablemate activities

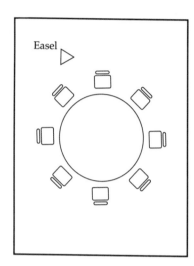

3. U-Shaped

- Ideal set-up for trainee performance or demonstration

- Works well for projections, media displays, and duo or team presentation using props and visual media

- Accommodates taping of participant's performance

- Works well for question/answer sessions when wishing to involve audience dialogue

- Allows for tablemates interaction, writing activities, and leader-led discussions

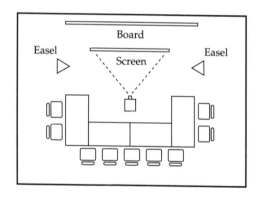

4. Fishbowl or Buzz Group

- Ideal for large groups of 30 or more

- Small group interaction possible with subgroups sitting at individual table

- "Fishbowl" layout is useful if you need to alternate entire group action with subgroup action

- Projection possible, but not the ideal set-up for this

- Each group can use easel and flipchart—and in total group sharing, charts can be taped up on the walls of the room

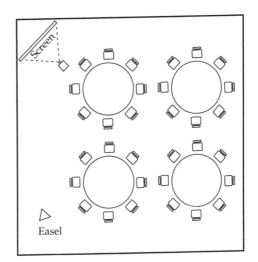

5. Role Play

- Allows for a large open center area in which to do role plays and still have total group visibility

- Allows observers to see action and then present reactions to total group

- Eliminates the need to keep moving furniture around to accommodate a variety of group activities

- Both writing and tablemate activities possible

- Allows camera shooting space for videotaping from one of the open areas

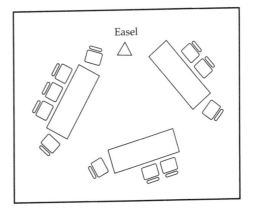

TIP #42 (continued)

6. V-Shaped

- Works well for showing movies or doing technical demonstrations

- Ideal for question/answer sessions

- Accommodates visuals for written testing activities

- Works well for peer/group performances like speechmaking

- Provides trainer with optimum view of total class when lecturing or demonstrating

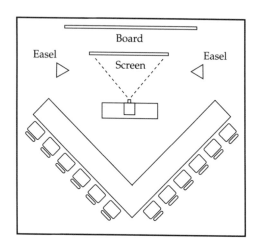

7. Conference Table

- Establishes a leadership position

- Accommodates group interaction for problem-solving sessions

- Provides total group a clear view of easel or board

- Does *not* accommodate projection viewing well or any type of role-playing activities

- Leader can see faces of all participants

- Can work well for informal or formal group activity

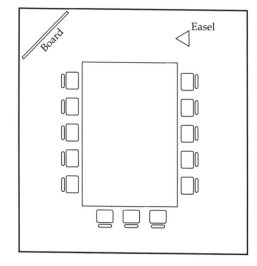

8. Production-Conference

- Functions well for action type meetings requiring discussion, writing, and projections

- With open end it can also work well for a formal speech presentation or demonstration

- When using extensive writing activity, trainer can move around the group easily to help individuals

- Works well for videotaping of group interaction since camera can be set up at open end of the table to view participants

- Works well for audio taping because microphone can be placed in the middle of the table to pick up all voices

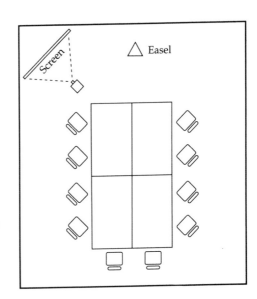

TIP #43 USE THIS TRAINING ROOM SET-UP FORM

Checklist:

Check the items that are required or are of concern to your presentation.

☐	Schoolroom	☐	Location of restrooms
☐	Roundtable	☐	Breaks scheduled
☐	Rectangle	☐	Refreshments
☐	Open or "U"	☐	Bar
☐	Buzz groups	☐	Coffee breaks
☐	_____		A.M. _____
☐	No. of Tables _____		P.M. _____
☐	No. of Chairs _____	☐	Security
☐	Any noise or other distractions?	☐	Coatroom
☐	Where is kitchen?	☐	Equipment checkout
☐	Windows	☐	Photography arrangement
☐	Lectern	☐	Press
☐	Stage	☐	Personal messages on door
☐	Sound proofing	☐	Meals
☐	Display tables	☐	How to pay bills
☐	Ventilation	☐	Guests
	Cooling _____	☐	Tips
	Heating _____	☐	Carpenter or electrical assistance
☐	Electric circuit check	☐	Departure procedures
☐	How to dim lights	☐	_____
☐	Special lighting	☐	_____
☐	Music	☐	_____

Now, list each item and what task is required in conjunction with it (for instance, tables taken down and chairs set in a semicircle). In the next column, write down whom you need to contact to see this gets done.

Item/Task	Person Responsible
1. _____	_____
2. _____	_____
3. _____	_____
4. _____	_____
5. _____	_____
6. _____	_____
7. _____	_____
8. _____	_____
9. _____	_____
10. _____	_____

SECTION

8

Select a Variety
of Media

USE A VARIETY OF TRAINING AIDS

A training aid is any device or piece of equipment that is used in the process of helping learners to comprehend the subject. Used properly, training aids enhance, support, and reinforce the subject matter and the trainer.

In addition to the audio-visual aids discussed earlier (films, video and audio-tapes, flipcharts, boards, and easels) there are many other training aids available:

- Overhead transparencies
- 35mm slides
- Tests

- Questionnaires
- Handouts
- Notebooks

For your training subject, which aids are most appropriate in the classroom setting? Which could you tailor for the trainee to keep after the course?

Classroom Aid	Take-Home
_____	_____
_____	_____
_____	_____
_____	_____
_____	_____
_____	_____
_____	_____
_____	_____

CHOOSE APPROPRIATE TRAINING AIDS

In planning training sessions, you should consider the possibility of clarifying difficult points with suitable illustrative materials.

Training aids may not lend themselves to every training situation, but when deemed appropriate, they should be made part of the presentation.

To determine if a training aid would be appropriate, consider your course content. Then ask yourself if an aid would be helpful in clarifying the subject matter. If so, then *what* aid would be most effective?

In considering visual training aids, the following may be considered as a guideline in selecting visuals. An effective training aid should be:

- Simple
- Legible
- Accurate

- Colorful
- Manageable
- Meaningful

Do you think his trainees will learn much from his training aids?

USE AIDS TO SUPPORT SPECIFIC OBJECTIVES

Visual aids should only be used to support a specific training objective—not as "eye-catchers" for boring training material. Keep the following in mind:

▶ Each visual should support a training concept taught within a learning unit.

▶ The information in each visual should relate directly to the verbal point being made by the trainer, leaving no confusion in the mind of the trainees.

▶ When using a series of visual aids, the aids would be presented in carefully planned order in accordance with lesson structure.

▶ Any color code, symbol, or lettering key should be visually displayed in the same manner in which the trainer verbally describes it during the lesson.

▶ Operation of the visual aid equipment or props should not interfere with what the trainer is saying to the group.

▶ When a visual begins to distract trainees from the learning objectives, then the visual aid is being misused and possibly interfering with the learning process.

▶ When planning the use of visual aids, the aids should be worked into the lesson plan and practiced prior to the actual session.

ORGANIZE YOUR AUDIO-VISUALS

Client: _____ Training Session: _____

Meeting Location: _____ Room No. _____

Date: _____ No. Attending: _____

Equipment Needed

☐ Cassette Recorder/Player
☐ Reel-to-Reel Tape Recorder
☐ Chalkboard
☐ Flipcharts/NO. _____
☐ Overhead Transparencies
☐ Transparencies
☐ Overhead Projector
☐ Record Player
☐ Opaque Projector Materials
☐ Extra Bulbs for equipment i.e., overhead projector
☐ Large screen for all to see
☐ Slide Projector
☐ Slides
☐ Filmstrip Projector
☐ Filmstrips
☐ 8mm Movie Projector
☐ 8mm Films

☐ 16mm Projector
☐ 16mm Films
☐ Sound/Slide Machines
☐ Slides and Tapes
☐ Video Cameras/Screen/Tripod
☐ Video Materials i.e., 1/2" VCR and large TV screen
☐ Masking Tape
☐ Computer
☐ Stage Lights
☐ Sound Systems
☐ Extension Cords
☐ Advertising Materials
☐ _____
☐ _____
☐ _____
☐ _____
☐ _____

Meeting Supplies

☐ Workbooks

☐ Notebooks

☐ Paper

☐ Pencils

☐ Attendance lists

☐ Water

☐ Chalk

☐ Large Badges

☐ Large Name Plates

☐ Large Markers
One set for each team _____

☐ Small Markers for transparencies
One set for each team _____

☐ _____

☐ _____

☐ _____

☐ _____

☐ _____

☐ _____

Other Notes:

_____

_____

_____

_____

_____

Prepared By: _____ **Submitted To:** _____

TAKE CARE OF PERSONAL ITEMS

► Have a supply of breath mints handy.

► Check your grooming and clothing carefully in a mirror before beginning the training.

ARRIVE ONE HOUR EARLY

Arrive at least one hour before the training session to arrange the room and organize all materials, including your own. *Do not* expose your audience to any housekeeping items related to the training. Be ready to start on time

PUT ON A SMILE AND HAVE FUN!

Leave your inappropriate moods at home or the office when you arrive at the training session. Try to enter the training with enthusiasm and energy even when you don't feel like it. Smile and personally greet the participants at the door with a handshake.

Have fun. If you have fun, your participants will also have fun!

DEVELOPING A PERSONAL ACTION PLAN

Think about the information in this book. What did you learn about yourself as a trainer? Where do you need to improve? Now, develop your personal action plan below:

1. My training skills are effective in these areas:

_____

_____

_____

_____

2. I have improved my teaching skills in the following areas:

_____

_____

_____

_____

3. My training skills need improvement in these areas:

_____

_____

_____

_____

4. I will evaluate my training skills in the following manner (describe how and when):

_____

_____

_____

_____

Your Signature: _____ **Date:** _____

ANSWERS: WORD SEARCH

Did you find all the words. Check your answers from page 57 with those circled below.

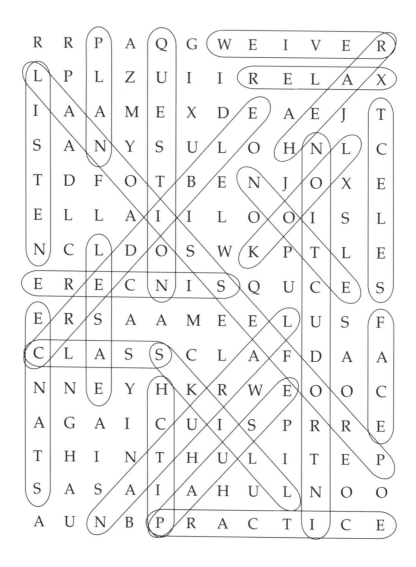

NOTES

NOTES

NOTES

NOTES

NOTES

NOTES

OVER 150 BOOKS AND 35 VIDEOS AVAILABLE IN THE 50-MINUTE SERIES

We hope you enjoyed this book. If so, we have good news for you. This title is part of the best-selling *50-MINUTE*™ *Series* of books. All *Series* books are similar in size and identical in price. Many are supported with training videos.

To order *50-MINUTE* Books and Videos or request a free catalog, contact your local distributor or Crisp Publications, Inc., 1200 Hamilton Court, Menlo Park, CA 94025. Our toll-free number is (800) 442-7477.

50-Minute Series Books and Videos Subject Areas . . .

Management
Training
Human Resources
Customer Service and Sales Training
Communications
Small Business and Financial Planning
Creativity
Personal Development
Wellness
Adult Literacy and Learning
Career, Retirement and Life Planning

Other titles available from Crisp Publications in these categories

Crisp Computer Series
The Crisp Small Business & Entrepreneurship Series
Quick Read Series
Management
Personal Development
Retirement Planning